In The Spirit:
Poems Of My Thoughts

Roots Of My Heart

M.D. SMITH

IN THE SPIRIT: POEMS OF MY THOUGHTS

ROOTS OF MY HEART

Scripture quotations marked KJV are from the Holy Bible, King James Version (Authorized Version). First published in 1611. Quoted from the KJV Classic Reference Bible, Copyright © 1983 by The Zondervan Corporation.

Scripture quotations marked NIV are taken from the Holy Bible, New International Version®. NIV®. Copyright © 1973, 1978, 1984 by International Bible Society. Used by permission of Zondervan. All rights reserved. [Biblica]

iUniverse books may be ordered through booksellers or by contacting:

iUniverse
1663 Liberty Drive
Bloomington, IN 47403
www.iuniverse.com
1-800-Authors (1-800-288-4677)

Because of the dynamic nature of the Internet, any web addresses or links contained in this book may have changed since publication and may no longer be valid. The views expressed in this work are solely those of the author and do not necessarily reflect the views of the publisher, and the publisher hereby disclaims any responsibility for them.

ISBN: 978-1-5320-3297-4 (sc)
ISBN: 978-1-5320-3298-1 (e)

Print information available on the last page.

iUniverse rev. date: 04/20/2018

COVER ART

SHONA STONE SCULPTURE
(Author's Personal Collection)

Origin: Shona People
            Great Zimbabwe • Central Southeast AFRICA

Composition: Black Serpentine – the hardest & darkest most commonly used for Shona carvings.
                (Existence: 2.6 billion years)

Cover Photography:
Michael E. Thomas • Photographic Dimensions

Photo Shoot Location:
Piano Craft Guild Gallery • Courtesy of Paul T. Goodnight & Bernice Robinson •
Color Circle Art Publishing, Inc.

In The Spirit:
Poems Of My Thoughts

Table of Contents

(i)

Author's Foreword
(Life Testimony)

"It's Been A Long Time Comin." *This is the title of one of my all-time favorite songs sung by The Winans and it's the sentiment of how I truly feel about the current stage of my life. Though I had a very "peachy keen" childhood that carried over to my graduation from college, my formative adult years, immediately following, were not pleasant. Specifically, the subsequent seven years after my European & USBL professional basketball career were not pleasant but rather deeply frustrating and perplexing. I didn't expect to experience what I did, given that I had successfully graduated from one of the best universities in the world along with history– making athletic achievements. However, "life on life's terms" was straight up in my face and I didn't respond well. All I had ever known was stellar academic & athletic achievement, no lacking of personal needs, and a loving/supportive/ close-knit circle of family & friends. I was truly blessed to have such a foundation. Yet, despite the seeming strength of that foundation, I ended up being shook to deep disbelief. The "big picture" just didn't add up. And then revelation, one day while crying out of frustration: "Wuz up, Lord?! I just don't understand. Am I doing something wrong? Please help me!!! And in His Great Compassion, My God heard my cry and attended unto my soul's deepest prayer —"Show me the way to my destiny, help me get there and maintain." I realized, in retrospect in 1990, that although I had always prayed before making any decisions, I was experiencing spiritual warfare —a battle with my spiritual enemy to realize my full potential and ordained life purpose. The serial attempts to obstruct and derail my ordained path by my spiritual enemy were persistent. Regardless, I determined to be even more persistent in defeating his assignment against me. Additionally, with my mind racing, energy ready to take on the next life challenge, the expectations to continue in the vein of personal success which came so easily for the first twenty-one years of my life, I(with the encouragement of a friend to attend N/A meetings) eventually realized the negative effects of my father's substance abuse illness on my life. The primary & profound point of information that I learned by hesitating then eventually attending a local 12- Step meeting is that substance abuse is a family illness. It directly impacts the user and indirectly impacts their loved ones in various ways. Upon consistently attending that N/A group meeting for one & one-half years, I realized that I had received all that N/A could give yet I still had some unresolved issues for which I strongly believed that I needed to address with a Christian counselor. Thankfully, my spiritual mother, Mary Elizabeth Langford Taylor was one (as her 2nd career; her first was as a RN). She helped me in the most profound & tremendous ways that eventually led to a major breakthrough and* *positioned me on the needed path of deep emotional & spiritual healing. My spiritual enemy didn't let up, though. In fact, he & his cohorts intensified their assault on my life — such that any positive progress that I shared with certain loved ones was met with a "hopeful but unconvinced response." This was deeply disheartening. Regardless, it was imperative (per my spiritual mother's wise counsel) that I continue to listen to God's prompting in my spirit and be obedient to following His Plan. Sadly, my dad's illness, prior to my Christian counseling, resulted in a "too early death" at the age of 54 due to denial of needing proper help. And his death on Oct. 4, 1996 will always be unpleasantly remembered given that the date is exactly (2) weeks after my birthday (Sept. 20th). The only good decision during that retrospection was that I was clear about "what's next?" after college graduation. As a result of a conversation with my assistant 6ball coach, Louise Foley, I joyfully submitted an application and was selected to tour w/Athletes In Action (Summer '86 • South America) and then returned to play a split continuum of professional basketball w/KFUM-Uppsala (1986) in Sweden and the United States Basketball League (1988-1992). After that, I honestly can't say that I was happy. Rollercoaster rides & waves of deep discouragement nagged me. My expectations were shot, job instability was prevalent, disappointment and frustration was my state of mind. I was on the verge of feeling hopeless that I'd never realize my adult life goals & dreams. And then, "Oh Happy Day," my breakthrough appeared after much agonizing prayer, crying, and sheer determination to fulfill my life purpose. The year was 1990, in Sept., when I sat down and wrote the business plan for my consulting business, Mission Possible: Collaborative (MP:C) and (at the time) its (2) subsidiaries, S.T.R.I.V.E. and M.D. Smith Publications. (* The 3rd subsidiary of MP:C, C.A.$.H., Inc., was birthed in 2006.) This was goin' to be the springboard to true professional joy, financial independence, and employment stability within my control. It was also the realization of my vision to be an entrepreneur & educator since age 14 — and it was. However, success came slowly — extremely slowly. Throughout the challenge of not earning enough to really live comfortably and having to supplement dba MP:C on a part-time basis while holding down a variety of jobs in the sectors of education, residential counseling, and youth development/services (that I truly enjoyed), The Lord reminded me that all that He ordained for me was going to happen in His Perfect Time not mine. Talk about feeling serially tested. So, what did I learn while I waited patiently (Psalm 40:1-17), continued to effectually & fervently pray (James 5:16) and hold firm to the great faith that my maternal grandmother said I had (Rom. 4:16,17b; II Corin. 4:7- 10; Phil 3:8-14, 4:6-9, 11-13; Heb. 11:1,6)? I learned to be a survivor & conqueror of my "faith-building tests, (Rom. 8:24-30, 35-39)" to really understand what it means to "totally depend on God"(Ps. 34:8, 141:8; Prov. 16:20b) and to enjoy the daunting challenge of "waiting patiently and with assured hope" (Ps. 34:19, 37:3-7, 9, 17b-19, 23-26; II Corin. 1:3-7, 20-22; 2:14; Eph. 3:14-21). And God says "This is only the beginning of 'your latter shall be greater.'"*

Well, that's it — what my long time comin' has been all about. Through the journey, I can genuinely claim the following as true:

(i) *"All things work together for good to them that love God and are called to His Purpose." (Rom. 8:28)*

(ii) *"I can do all things through Christ who strengthens me." (Phil. 4:13)*

(iii) *"Be not weary in well doing; for in due season, you will reap if you do not faint." (Gal. 6:9)*

Great Is The Lord

He created the world, He is the giver of life.

He gave his only begotten Son, Jesus,

that we may have life in a new light.

He wants us to do His will, and if our souls we empty,

He promises His Holy Spirit will fill.

His greatest promise is "I will never leave you, nor forsake you."

The Lord is great to me, yes, because in my life

He guides me through.

I love the Lord with all my heart, soul, and mind;

and in my daily service, to Him, this will I prove.

Why Did You Do It?

Jesus, you say you died for the sins of the world —

but why? So that we may live abundantly — but how?

By carrying on the Word of God

through our individual God-given talents — but why?

To build up the kingdom of God

and secure our place in life everlasting — to do what?

Rejoice in the Almighty God, our Father for all that He did,

does, and will do forever more.

Well, Jesus, I'm so glad you did it all.

True Living

My definition of true living?

My soul is care-free, it is occupied by an exciting Spirit.

My mind is worry-free and focused on high-level optimism.

My true identity exposes itself from within me.

My sense of true living is knowing

that the Spirit within me is alive and eternal.

My mind is focused on Jesus Christ as I strive to be like Him.

And, my body is like potter's clay, it is being molded into shape by God.

All of me is in the maturing process…to be perfected by God for His use.

Thus, I will yield to His direction for me which has been ordained

since the beginning of time.

Yes, this for me, is true living.

Sing Unto The Lord
(A Hymn)

The time has come. Ev-ery-one needs to give God the praise.
Let us gi--ve glor-y to Him on hi--gh. Praise him, for it is
the Power, Power of God, th--at will gi--ve tru-e lib-er-ty...
Oh, oh, oh, o-o-o-oh (echo).

Chorus #1 (2x):

For all that He does (2x), praise Him (2x).
Lift up your voice (2x), and sing unto The Lord

Verse (Repeat)

Chorus #2 (2x):

For who He is (2x), worship Him (2x).
He's the Most High (2x), so sing unto The LORD.

Fade Out (Chorus #1, #2)

Happiness Is…

Happiness, in my vocabulary, is analogous to blessedness.

And blessedness or being blessed is a gift from God to us

shown in infinite ways. Just to be able to breathe, talk, hear,

walk, see a new day and the list is never ending.

Yes, in all of God's blessings, there is a touch of joy He brings.

Whether our blessedness be in small or large measures,

we ought to be rejoicing.

So, let us get in-tuned to be thankful to God

who continuously blesses us, and then you'll really realize that

Happiness is Blessedness.

Life Is A Blessing

Many people complain about how hard it is to cope;

yet others just hold onto faith and hope.

I don't understand how and why, at times, folk get depressed;

'cause I just thank God for each day that I live and I know I'm blessed.

There's so much beauty in being alive;

so just hang on in there, persevere and thrive.

All of us can truly make it with the help and use of Gods Armor & Spirit.

God, He can supply your every need;

your hungry soul, He will feed.

Yes, truly I believe—life is a blessing, indeed;

if you live by faith, faith as a grain of mustard seed.

African Consciousness

African people: be confident and rejoice in the richness of your African heritage.

Do not, do not deny the roots of your culture and history.

Be conscious of what it means to be a descendent of African ancestors.

*Find your own place in the many environments of this world. Keep your mind
focused on solid knowledge, knowledge of self and personal purpose in this life.*

There is no way for us black people to change our conditions of existence,

unless we keep on in the struggle

for social, economic, and political equality. We must be persistent.

All African people must realize the need to be supportive and united

in our discovery of true freedom. May the Living God who has helped us

to endure many hardships through time, give us everlasting spiritual, mental,

physical strength and wisdom to move on and upward.

And, let our minds be in accord with the Creator that we may always reach

for a perpetual discovery of power as many but one African consciousness.

The Word Is Out

Did you hear that The Word is out? If you are clueless to

what I am referring to — listen closely. What I am going to convey

in this message is not gossip or back-talking. The Word that I speak about

is of a mighty power. It is pure, honest, an educational.

The Word is God's Word, the Holy Bible.

If one holds onto and practices this Word, the rewards are rich and infinite.

Just give The Word a try. There is no guarantee that changes will happen
immediately. However, if you are willing to adhere and persevere

with the knowledge of The Word, blessings will come in time — abundantly.

The best way to benefit from this Word is to get a hold of it, meditate on it,

and effectively apply it. It is a lifetime task but the effort to seek and discover the truth

and beauty of this Word is worth the sacrifice, 'cause it is one that, forever, will last.

God And I

The Lord God and I have come to be close. This is so through our
personal relationship that uniquely only He & I know.

My relationship with God and His family is everlasting and tight.

I warn anyone who tries to destroy these most valuable friendships;

if you dare try, we will fight.

God is my Best Friend, He is always present when I praise, pray, and call Him.

He hears and answers to my every need, and not 'cause I do any great deeds.

I just have to obey and act on God's Word, and He will bless my life abundantly.

Every day I praise God with invaluable sincerity as He allows me to see a new day.

I plan to always follow in the paths of righteousness

as He gives me strength.

God and I, we can do anything, there is no limit.

My guide and strength is--- the Holy Spirit.

For My Brothers And Sisters

We must recognize our societal history and self/collective purpose in this life

and support each other in daily living.

There is no power greater than the spiritual force which can bind us and

keep us in line with our walk as a people persevering to thrive.

The Living God is a Source of Strength for all people.

We must be servants of God in representing ourselves as peaceful, loving persons

as He wants us to be. The rewards of acting as such will be great.

No matter how much we try to do on our own, we'll never be able to match

what God can do for us in His power, alone.

So, I say to you my brothers and sisters:

If you feel that your efforts to create aren't producing any results,

please consider a new plan, God's plan. Why? God has everything in limitless

stock. So, let us come to believe God for lifting us up where we belong.

With whole-hearted desire to seek and follow God's will

for our self/collective purpose, a coming change will not be long.

In fact, in knowing that God has and always will provide a way out of no way,

we can be overcomers, victorious, every day.

The Angelic Dove

What peace and gentleness it portrays!

It travels curiously through the sky;

it searches for a place in nature's wonderland to claim as home.

As we search to find our place in divine destiny, may we soar high as does
the dove. May peace, joy, and love---characteristics of the dove,

be your ways to thrive in whatever you do.

And yes, for all you strive to do, this poem is for you.

Souled Out For Jesus

Life is a blessing for sure; and in Jesus' hands it's guaranteed secure.

On our own, there's only so much we can do, we have limits.

So, all the more reason for Jesus to be eternally present in our souls as the Holy Spirit.

If we sell out for Jesus, what blessings...

there's so many incorruptible riches He will endow.

Our part in this most awesome deal is to submit ourselves and be for real.

This most precious decision of how to live your life; it's an eternal commitment.

So as I live for Jesus, I tell you all:

If you decide to live for Him, there's only one way to do it...

be persistent.

Let Jesus Be Your Best Friend

A friend is a person that we all cherish and love.

It's a privilege that God gives us to have friends, even if we only ever have one.

And the Best Friend that God could have ever given us is His Son.

Jesus is a special friend, a friend like no other.

He's so close and dear, we can claim Him also as our heavenly brother.

Jesus, He's always there when you need Him.

He helps in the good times, the bad times, the hard times.

He'll never leave you nor forsake you.

And the greatest part of letting Him be your Best Friend is,

unconditionally, Jesus loves you too.

Friendship Is…

Friendship Is….   that special bond of love amongst peers.

Friendship ….   it's about being with your special someone(s), sharing good cheer.

Friendship Is….   confiding in someone you know you can trust, to give advice or other help in time of need.

Friendship Is….   giving to each other, to the spirit and to the soul, food to feed.

Friendship Is….   being there in the good times and the bad times, the sad and the glad.

Friendship Is….   being comforted when you've had all you can have.

Friendship Is….   a relationship in which love strengthens, care abounds, and nothing can force it to separate or be bent.

Friendship Is….   a gift, a God-given privilege that's Heaven sent.

Give An Effort

Racism and stubbornness are two attitudes that I can't stand.

What is wrong is this: people who have either of these (2) temperaments,

they just don't take time to understand.

I mean why pre-judge or turn away from "socializing"

because of race and/or color.

Why not give an effort to communicate with everyone

like you would with a sister and/or brother.

There's no reason, no none, for all people to not give a try in getting along.

So, be open to meeting others without pre-meditated conceptions

and don't make excuses to prolong.

Give an effort, always in life, in everything you do.

'Cause you never know, especially in "socializing",

what chances a friendship may develop

or, at least, others have the pleasure to meet you.

Power Of The Will

As the saying goes, and it's true, "you can do anything you want to do."

This is so, especially, if that something is beneficial, and of great value to you.

There are times, though, when your mind can hinder your doings because of doubt.

But do not fret because there is always available help from God, the sure way out.

No matter what the circumstances of your situation, God's power can (without fail)

always be counted the sure thing.

Pure happiness, strength, peace, and love to your soul He will bring.

So when facing reality,

remember that power of the will is always a winner — guaranteed.

To Love And Be Loved

It is said that "life is an experience" of give and take.

And the success of happiness and direction in your life

is really in what of it you make.

There is one need though that without it nothing in life can truly be right.

And that one must is that to love and be loved shine super bright.

A perfect example of love is that of the man known as Jesus Christ.

So bright, always, did His love for others shine

that He was amongst many names known as "The Light."

Don't ever be afraid to show love towards anyone.

'Cause at least in wanting to express love, God's first and greatest commandment

to love all people is fulfilled.

Yes, to love and be loved is as beautiful if not better than the
season presence of Spring. So always sow to reap love

because in the long run, an infinity of spiritual blessings the effort will bring.

Be A Winner

You say life is hard, nothing but a massive headache? So, you feel down and out?

Sure, times can be tough but good news; God's help is always available

and your problems you can "shout out".

Don't let anything or anyone put you down.

Know the Lord is your power and stand up on high and higher ground.

Victory in life you can always have when you have God on your side.

So don't give into temptation and be tossed and turned like a water's tide.

Be a winner always...with God's help no problem,

you can stand for what's right.

And thus, you'll always be a positive role model to others

as you stand firm in the Lord's sight.

My Favorite Sport

Sports. Whether participating in low or high competition,

there's no better way, in my opinion to feel good about physical exercise.

And yes, if you are consistent in the sport of your choice,

very likely, you'll feel better about your health and to do so is wise.

One of the best sports, for an all-out good sweat, and one referred to

as "the ultimate team sport" is basketball.

Basketball is a game where I.Q. and talent must be proved.

And as one gives time to practice, eventually, their game will improve.

Basketball is a game of 5 on 5.

And it is very important that each member of a team gives 100+% effort,

which means always try, try, try.

Basketball is my favorite sport because I learned to play at my best and how to win.

I receive great joy, also, because you share wins and losses with those folks

who are your teammates.

So, for all of these reasons, to me, the sport of basketball is the greatest.

Music Of The Soul

There are many varieties of music and all have a message ;

but the best melodies to me are gospel and jazz —

music that is (in true form) oh so whole.

Gospel or Christian songs go way back to the earliest of days

and impart joy, peace, and inspiration to the soul.

And Jazz is music of many different facets but its origin is African.

There's traditional, New Orleans style, cool, contemporary, bebop, Big Band,

and improvisational.

However, jazz originated later than gospel in time (about the late 1800's).

So, here you have it — a brief summation of the music

with ancient but oh so live rhythm.

Gospel and Jazz, Jazz and Gospel, my spirit dances with 'em.

The Beauty Of Nature

Have you ever thought about what life would be like

without the beauty of nature?

If there were no birds, no plant life,

no serene or cool winds, streams, lakes, rivers, or seas?

If there were no animals and oh no way

to reproduce the precious value of human life itself?

Why then everything would be lifeless like a toy doll sitting on a shelf.

Life without the beauty of nature is not a colorful life;

and all that existed in this type of world, would be void of some highlights.

But you see, God who created the universe

felt that Creation had to be pleasant to sight.

Thus, when He spoke the world into existence, He made sure it was done quite nice.

Oh, how wonderful is the beauty of nature; how I love it so.

And how great it is that it was so carefully created and its warmth and glory show.

Dialogue: A Day Spent With Jesus

Scene 1:   Jesus has called on me to spend a day with Him.

Intro: Jesus and I are deciding what is to be the activity of the day.

Jesus: Well, Michelle, it really doesn't matter to me what we do as long as it's fun. In fact, I'll do what you want to do.

Me: Well, Jesus, I must say I do have a particular activity in mind.

Jesus: What is it?

Me: How 'bout a game of basketball, one-on-one? Of course as you know, Our Father has given me natural talent as an all-around athlete. But, it was my desire to glorify Him as a basketball player. And, of course, I know He gave you all the talent there is in the world. So, what do you say?

Jesus: Sure, let's play! I believe this will be a challenge for both of us and it'll be fun.

Scene 2:   Enter Jesus and I on a super, smooth basketball court, one of the best there is.

Me: How do you want to start the game, Jesus? Your ball or mine?

Jesus: You start the game, Michelle.

Me: Thanks, I believe I'm gonna need all the breaks I can get.

Jesus: What?! You're a great player! Remember, you were born with the talent from above.

Me:	So, were you. Well, here goes. (The game starts with a check to Jesus.) I score the first point with a fake, then a drive to the hoop. The game is to 7 by 1(s).
Jesus:	Good move, Michelle. Score 0-1 Check, then Jesus...up for a high rise jump shot. Score 1-1.
Me:	The move: a fake, pull-up jump shot. Score 2-1.
Jesus:	A quick step... stop... reverse direction... pull-up jumper. Score 2-2.
Me:	A quick step to the hoop...bank shot. Score 3-2.
Jesus:	A dribble to the left...to the right, then a crossover down the left lane, and in for a lay-up. Score 3-3.
Me:	A quick jumper from the free throw line. Score 4-3.
Jesus:	A quicker jumper than my last one, at the corner of the free throw line. Score 4-4.
Me:	A dribble left, right, left, pull-up jumper with left hand. Score 5-4.
Jesus:	An attempt, no a real high speed drive to the hoop...too fast for me that time. Score 5-5.
Me:	A dribble right, left, right, up with a finger roll lay-up off of a 180° turn. Score 6-5.
Jesus:	A dribble right, left, right, a 360° turnaround 10 ft. jumper. Score 6-6.

(This Is It!, Tie Score...Game Point)

| Me: | A dribble left, right, pull-up jumper. Oh, no! It doesn't fall in! (rolls around the rim then off) |

Jesus: *Gets the rebound, clears the ball over the free throw line. For 1 minute, I play tight defense. Jesus makes no move to score. But then, Jesus dribbles left, then right, then left again into a 360° turn and reverse slam dunk. What a point!*

FINAL SCORE: Jesus - 7, Me - 6

Me: *Great game, Jesus (exhausted), especially that last point. How...?*

Jesus: *As it is written: "As the heavens are higher than the earth, so are my ways higher than your ways" (Isaiah 55:9) (This is the answer to how Jesus jumped so high on that last point despite my slim advantage in physical height.)*

(** <u>Note</u> : The game bein' to 7 was especially inspirational to Jesus since the number "7" is "the biblical number of completion.")*

Communication: An Absolute Necessity

There is something very special that all people share

and cannot do without. And, that is communication,

it's an absolute necessity...this no one can doubt.

Do you realize how important it is to express yourself to others?

It's "super important" to be comfortable in sharing how you feel

or having a one-on-one with someone who'll understand sincerely.

I'd say what a comfortless, boring world it would be —

no one listening, observing, or caring to take time to be.

Regardless, realize that you are responsible for your communication,

You must persist 'til you've said what you need to say,

and communication between you and all who you know becomes what it should.

Perfection: An Ultimate Goal

Perfection. How is it reached, and then how does it become a personal constant?

Is the old proverb: "practice makes perfect", the way?

I say rather it's "perfected practice makes perfect."

I'm sure for different people, there are different definitions of perfection.

For me, there is only one way to strive for and attain perfection —

as said by my dear friend Todd Cotton —

"Strive for perfection in everything you think, say, and do."

Without a doubt, perfection in a skill or skills is a worthy goal to pursue.

I believe it's quite a goal to be reached, don't you?

B.L.E.S.S.E.D.

B   *is for being born-again...oh the greatness of its*
transforming power.

(II Corinthians 5:17)

L   *is for the Love of God, without it no one would*
feel safe knowing God, as a refuge, a strong tower.

(John 3:16, 17; Psalm 46:1)

E   *is for edification, it is the nourishment that helps*
us to grow up toward perfection in Christ.

(Ephesians 4:10-16)

S   *is for sanctification. True holiness is what it's*
about. The example to follow is Christ, the only
way to do it right.

(I Peter 1:16)

S   *is also for servant. Serve the Lord for the reward is*
sweet, and life in His service is truly upbeat.

(Colossians 3:23, 24)

E   *is also for excitement. Think about Jesus and what*
He can do through you. You'll see if you yield
yourself continually and to Him be true.

(II Timothy 2:20, 21)

D   *is for diligence in everything you say and do. To*
do anything successfully, you must in Christ's
strength, follow through.

(John 15:5, Philippians 4:13)

Life: A Precious Gift

The gift of life is such a privilege, such an infinitely diverse

spectrum of experiences.

Is there anything that can compare to the awesomeness of life?

Life, when the Creator spoke it into existence,

brought about the great miracle known as birth.

And in all that dwells in Heaven and Earth as birth, there is

a time of season, a season to which there is a special reason.

We are living examples of a physical and spiritual being

created in the image of the Creator. Thus, we have times of seasons,

a purpose to our lives, special reasons.

The Creator's creation are we, the we with seasons, missions,

destinations with reasons.

Let us walk boldly and powerfully in the likeness of the Creator.

Life is a precious gift, a gift of freedom

given by the Creator to us that are born of His Spirit.

So rejoice and live rejuvenated;

'Cause life is a precious gift that's been given to you.

So, through the power of the Creator's Spirit, live it!

A Time For Everything

In the Book of Ecclesiastes, Chapter 3, Verse 1,

it is written: "To everything there is a season, and a time to every purpose

under Heaven."

Fact: This is an all-inclusive statement meaning there is a time for all things.

So if you acknowledge that there is a time for everything,

and you accept and walk in that truth,

Is there not confirmation that whatever happens in your life is that truth

now become proof?

Now, this confirmation I must say is only the beginning.

The real test lies in what will you do about knowing that there is a time

for everything, for everything a season, a reason?

Will you deal or not deal when, in your life, times are bad and sad?

I sincerely encourage you to face the bittersweets,

'cause through persevering your faith will be strengthened,

and you'll experience victories.

And when the opportunity arises, bless others by sharing how you

(in your trials and tribulations) were brought through.

Thus, in there being a time for everything, and for everything that happens

a reason, this should we do---(I Thessalonians 5:18):

"In everything give thanks: for this is the will of God in Christ Jesus concerning you."

Ups And Downs

There is a saying: "No pain, no gain". And sometimes in life,

we forget about what that means.

In other terms it can be said,

we must in our lives be exposed to "the sunshine and the rain".

You say why not just give me the good, forget about the bad.

And as well, I want only to be glad never sad.

Wait...take a moment and reflect on "the valley and mountaintop" experiences

in your life.

Have you not so much the more appreciated the blessings

of "going through to get through?"

If your answer to this question is yes, true,

then whatever happens in your life; you'll understand to a point

when you'll say: "Oh, that's nothing new."

So, rejoice in your sorrows and joys, your ups and downs.

For in doing so, you'll be a witness to others

and in someone's time of need(s), be a friend, a comfort, a joy to be around.

Perfect Peace

There is a calmness, a loud quietness in the only peace

that surpasses all understanding...the peace of God.

It is so awesome that at times it's even "odd".

I mean how is it that when challenges

of all kind come your way, and there's no one visible to turn to,

God is always there to say:

"Hey, I can take that burden, that pain far away".

How is it that if you look to the great "I Am", He can restore your spirit?

Well, God gives an answer to this question.

He says:

"Thou wilt keep him in perfect peace, whose mind is stayed on thee:

because he trusteth in thee." (Isaiah 26:3)

Thus, no matter what's happenin' in your life or around you,

you can experience peace with God, peace of God and be free.

Don't Worry

Why be concerned about your past and/or your future?

Why not live moment by moment, day by day, in the present.

'Cause, you see, those other time frames they're gone away and a while away.

So, don't worry.

Set your mind on doing that which is before you, forgetting what is behind.

You can do it, overcome, despite whatever the odds against you.

When you've worked so hard at something, gone so far,

and somehow your efforts seem like nothing at all.

Don't worry.

When there's a pile of bills you must face, your finances are low,

and the only words you can say are "ought oh, oh no."

Don't worry.

When in your life you're going through, you don't know what to do?

Don't worry, but instead know this:

God cares and all of your burdens He'll faithfully share.

So, don't worry, don't worry ever.

'Cause what concerns you and that means...in all things,

God will (if you let Him) be your everything.

What Is, Where Is, Who Is Black America?

What Is Black America?

Is the term "Black America" well-distinguished?

It can be generally defined as the group of colored skin people

of various black cultural heritages who live in the U.S.A.

Well, that description is clear and distinctive, isn't it??

So, where is Black America? As far as I know, there is no specific location.

In reminiscence, life for blacks in America wasn't so hot for the first 400 years.

Ya know why? 'Cause they were forced to reside and work in this Land

as slaves for white, racist European colonists...shackled and shipped to the U.S.A.
in horrendous conditions, against their will from their homes far and near.

It's true! Black People do not have their cultural roots in North America;

even though some of us have generations of our families who have been here for a while.

We're still seeking equality through a continual journey of "proverbial long miles."

And, who is Black America?

Are the members worthy of the group only those who have set precedent

for progress of the black race (e.g. Benjamin Banneker, George Washington Carver,
Charles Drew, Sojourner Truth, Harriet Tubman, Mary McLeod Bethune, Ida B.
Wells, Madame C.J. Walker; W.E.B. DuBois, Stokely Carmichael (aka Kwame Ture),
Marva Collins, MLK, Jr., Malcolm X, Barbara Jordan, Rev. Jesse L. Jackson, etc.)

Or is it, as I know it's suppose to be, the collection of black people

who make up the entire race? Yes, it's the collection that is Black America.

So, why are there so many hidden faces? Why is there chism in the body of people

that are descendants of kings & queens?

Why are there classes (i.e. black bourgeoisie, upper & middle class, working class, and poor)

of black folk who are so disunited from being a united, uplifted black race?

It's time to come together—a black race that truly supports its members as a whole.

Calling all people of African descent: open your eyes, open your eyes.

Let us move up in establishing ourselves as people who truly stand up, stand beside,

look out for each other. My prayer is that some day soon

we'll be truly living united as sisters and brothers.

I Have All Things

Whatever I need, whatever I want, I get it 'cause Gods got it.

To understand what I mean you must know that the Word of God

is Truth. You see I have all things because in Psalm 24:1 it says:

"The earth is The Lord's and the fullness thereof; the world,

and they that dwell therein." See God created and therefore possesses control

over everything that is matter.

And since I am a child of God, an heiress to all His spiritual blessings

and a joint heiress to His Kingdom, I receive from above

and hence enjoy becoming spiritually fatter.

The Almighty, Living God, my Heavenly Father

is the richest of the rich, He lacks in nothing.

Therefore, I always receive from Him all of my necessary and desired somethings.

I'm so blessed to be able to say that I have all things,

but it's no special privilege that's exclusive. You can have all things, too.

All it takes to be "truly rich" is to be connected to the only Living God,

the best Father a person could have, as your source of wealth.

That's all, seriously, that's all you have to do.

So, why not get it for yourself?

Giving Honor: When And To Whom It Is Due
(Romans 13:7)

All people are gifted with something(s) that they do well.

And there are people who positively influence

our individual lives and help us to develop into a mature, strong person.

Through giving advice, sharing, sacrificing self, and fellowship,

we receive from these people, learning lessons.

It is to them (mothers, fathers, sisters, brothers, close friends, ministers)

that we should give heartfelt thanks for what they have given us.

Better yet, all honor and glory should be given to the Living God for it is only just.

The reason being is that it is the Lord who has created individuals

so original and with such beautiful talents that they may give of themselves to His glory.

In fact, He encourages us to be these type of people in the Old and New Testament

of the Bible, in the form of true stories.

So, as we live this life, may we always remember

to give honor when and to whom it is due.

*And prioritize: you should praise God first and then give loving
thanks to those others who are special and there for you.*

So Worthy To Be Praised
(A Song)

Lord, for who you are and all you do and have done;

I'll continually praise you from the rising to the setting of the sun.

You grant me peaceful sleep every night;

you wake me with new mercies every morning.

My soul sings with joy whether the day is cloudy or brightly shining.

Your peace is perfect, your joy is my strength; my strength

and as your child all of your spiritual blessings are mine.

Father, Son, and Holy Spirit you're always there for me;

you're everything, forever so divine.

Chorus (2x):

Worthy, worthy, you're so worthy to be praised

From the rising of the sun to the setting of the same;

Lord, I'll continually praise your name.

Verse (Repeat)

Chorus (Repeat)

Fade Out: From the rising of the sun to the setting of the same:

Lord, I'll continually praise your name.

A Determined, Talented Man

He is young, cultured, sensitive, and has a down-to-earth spirit

and these traits make him the loveable person he is.

The career pursuit is acting, writing, and producing---the whole realm of showbiz.

No, this isn't impossible for Erik Todd Dellums nor is it too ambitious.

For God has given him a natural talent for all 3; he's working extremely hard

'cause he wants to be the best he can be.

Erik is dear to me in a special way; he's my 2nd best male friend.

And through our college years at Brown, we shared many happy times,
most excitingly, our destiny, goals to achieve and live to their end.

For Erik, as stated, the 3 areas of his fine arts;

for me---entrepreneur/teacher, mentor, writer

and we're both at the same place---progressive pursuit, doing it successfully.

So, onward press we will 'til we taste sweet victory.

A determined, talented man, ETD is for sure.

I'll continue to admire and pray for his inevitable success

and look forward to us rejoicing when "we have arrived" to say:

"Thank you God, family, and friends. We did it, oh yes!!!"

What An Example

You are my greatest earthly examples of unconditional love —

always there for me, present or in spirit. The Lord always granted you the ability

to provide my needs and wants; the blessing being unconditional giving.

You taught me to "do unto others as you would have them do unto you."

Your encouragement has always been constant through my times

of decision, trial, and pursuit of accomplishments — so true blue.

Always when needed, prayer and words of wisdom

flowed from you in support of my efforts to strive for excellence in everything.

The sense of humor and all that you are has continually brought joy, laughter,

and sense of reality — causing my soul to sing.

Your faith in the Lord is never ceasing, though at times shaken;

it has resulted in shaping who I am in Christ and from His presence

I know I can never be taken.

So for all that you've done and said, do and say, will do and will say;

God bless you exceeding and abundantly above all that you ask or think in this life.

May I be as great if not a greater inspiration to others as you continue to be to me.

The results? I'll trust and see.

Shining Star

You're a shining star, twinkling ever so bright.

You have it all because Jesus is your Guiding Light.

What amazes me is that we have a common, covenant bond; you're just as you are.

And your God-given talents are going to take you far.

Emmanuel, "The Lord Be With You", will always be your constant companion.

He'll see you through all of your seasons and while there it will be revealed:

Yes, that's the reason.

The fullness of your inheritance, the greatest of all, awaits your desire to claim.

Be bold, strong, full of God's Word and never give up; you're destined for "fame".

You'll always come out on top with the Lord on your side.

So continually walk in faith; and in Him, abide.

Be Not Overwhelmed?!

Be Not Overwhelmed?! Be Not Overwhelmed?!

I say, I say: "when my heart is overwhelmed, lead me to The Rock

that is higher than I."

How can I unload when the weight is so heavy

and you don't seem nigh?

I know it won't be happenin' in my power;

But through me, 'cause You're The Source—The Strong Tower.

At times, though, I'm pressed — losing my grip,

can't get loose from what has my spirit down.

So, I call you —The Very Present Help

and we experience footprints to The Higher Ground.

Life in this world is a serious trip;

every now and then it has me undesirably spinning;

but ever grateful that in You, I'm an overcomer, winning.

Thank-you Lord, in the midst of daily living,

for the gift of sound mind.

Your comforting words: "be not overwhelmed," embrace me;

for I am thine.

Unity

There is such an awesome power in agreement that can set us on the highest plains.

So why does conflict of interests, destruction through all types of wars

continue to plague, causing immense pain?

This is so because there's not enough pure courage, faith, and fighting spirit

in our neighborhoods, in our world to make the needed change.

What happened? Why is so much crime going down, out of control?

We let our guard down, fear began to reign, now we must recapture

all that was stole.

We've lost confidence, determination, effort, love, respect, and sincerity of soul.

We can't afford to keep traveling this road.

So, let's get our act together — desiring to be straight.

The time is way overdue, no longer can we wait.

Only through unconditional unity will we conquer and stand to see no more

the extreme cases of diseases that have us bound:

fear, racism, and all others.

We must become one, a stable and unstoppable force,

like an impenetrable cover.

D.E.S.T.I.N.Y.

We all are called to an ultimate place to be; it's called your life's calling, your destiny. And this is how ya get there —successfully:

D   *for Determination*

E   *for Excellence in everything you do*

S   *for Surrender to God's will for your life (which is your true heart's desire, anyway)*

T   *for Tenacity — no matter what, keep the faith and press on*

I   *for Imagination — set no limit to all that you can be & do*

N   *for Nurture your faith, your dreams*

Y   *for Yearning — persistently pursuing what's ahead*

Roots Of My Heart

Table of Contents

(i)

New Beginnings

A new day had begun. The sun arose with exceptional brilliance, the sky was clear, and the sounds of nature were loud and near. It was one of those "perfect" days; but for some reason, today was going to be somewhat different.

The gang was psyched to do the usual: go to school, cut up during recess, and hang out at Classic Video after school. "Will we always do the same thing," said Jamie. No one responded; it seemed that everyone else was just not there. Observing all the beauty of the day, peter said, "Man, this is a beach-type day. I don't want to really do the usual with the gang. I'm gonna stay outside and cool out. Yeah!" Jill, John, and Elise came along boppin' down the street to meet up with the gang. And as they walked, they thought: "Wow, today is really nice! October weather in New England is rarely ever 75 degrees. Let's do something outside and fun for a change." So, they went off to the park with a frisbee and played ultimate frisbee.

At this point, everyone in the gang was off doing what they wanted. Jamie, Peter, Jill, John, and Elise were making the most of this unusually, delightful day. "I enjoyed being by myself. I went bike riding in the breeze. I wonder what the rest of the gang did," thought Jamie. Peter, who was totally submerged in hangin' out, pondered "I like doing something different once in a while, even though I'm into time with the gang." And the threesome that went to the park, they just experienced fun like never before. Jill, John, and Elise enjoyed being in the open field — running, playing, being silly.

When the gang did get together the next day, they all agreed that it was nice to take a break from each other. The more that they ventured doing other things of interest, the more they enjoyed it: making new friends, being alone, doing and learning new ways to have fun, maturing.

Jamie, Peter, Jill, John, and Elise remained friends regardless of how often they got together. As to what other events happened that developed the gang's friendship and their individual characters, well...

Do What You Can

Your knowledge, your resources, your time are limited.
You want to do more than you're able; but 'til increase comes,
you have to do with what you have.
Keep strechin' and usin' what you possess, and God will take care of the rest.
Say you can't do much because you don't know how;
Do what you do know and eventually you'll learn more.

Do what you can and do it in the very best way.
Don't be anxious about doing all that you want
'cause it will all come together — someday.

A loved one is feeling sad and alone.
You've tried to cheer up but nothing seems to comfort.
There is no joy you discover.
So now that you know why, you can specifically intercede on their behalf
By praying for God's cover.

Don't get in a situation where it'll be over your head.
Be patient and just hang in there with God;
by His Spirit, always be led.

Do what you can and do it in the very best way.
Don't be anxious about doing all that you want
'cause it will all come together — someday.

Covenant Sacrifice

The devotion to our common bond needs to grow stronger and stronger.
Without a second thought, we must get to the point where sharing all our goods
is not a problem any longer.
As we cheerfully give our tithes and hold each other up,
The Lord will multiply — filling our cups.
There will not be enough room to receive what He'll pour out;
If we just go His way, we'll see His blessings stay.

Obey and be ready to provide a covenant sacrifice.
When it's in our power to supply a need, let's willingly heed.

To give of yourself is not drudgery, if you see that it is adding "sunshine"
to an otherwise dull day.
By giving, you will be released from your binds;
you're now one step closer to having Christ's mind.

Obey and be ready to provide a covenant sacrifice.
When it's in our power to supply a need, let's willingly heed.

The Time Is Now

There always is talk in our society about what could be, should be,
would be, and is; but there never seems to be enough commitment to act for change,
short-term or long range.
There are a few reasons, observed, for why change doesn't happen:
* fear of failure, being worst off than before
* not knowledgeable about the needed resources
or knowing and running into closed doors
* "passing the buck", not focusing on the core of the issue.

Why such a vicious cycle?
Why don't people catch the vision of where the power lies?
It's in their hands to adamantly communicate their concerns & ideas
and then seek the solution with their mind.
In troublesome times, we must not hesitate to stand firm in our beliefs and values.

We can't let the present hinder us from having a healthy future.
So, let's step out in faith and with unbroken stride, armed with the attitude:
we'll be problem solvers, determined to win our fights.

Do You Know Why?

The youth of today need to be cautious about "doing their own thang."
Do you know why?
Some say it's cool, dope, hype to hang in the streets
and learn how to make quick money, big time.
Yet, the frequent scenario – violence, jail, death ; then hangin' ain't worth a dime.
Do you know why the dealing and violence goes on and on?
It's 'cause the attitude is: "I'll never get caught. Nothing is gonna happen to me."
Yet, eventually, they discover that they were fooling themselves
and the truth becomes plain and seen.
Family, friends, neighbors – all hurt by living where there is no sense of hope.
Safety, trust, and values just aren't in order. What to do?
We must join in boldly reclaiming our cities from coast to coast.
Wherever youth are dying from street life, they must be given alternatives
that in the long run won't cause strife.

Parents, teachers, government, and others concerned must push to save this generation
for the sake of our future.
Youth need to see opportunities to thrive the old-fashioned & lasting way:
get an education and then work honestly to earn your pay.
Of course, the youth have their part: they must choose to live rather than to die.
Pray that the strays will come to their senses:
desiring peace vs. violence, unity vs. division, love vs. hate
and wholeheartedly say "Later streets, goodbye."
To preserve our youth, we must answer the questions:
Do you know why?

Provision Is In The Source

We all have need to be stable: emotionally, spiritually, and to be steadfastly strong.
Where can you go to receive? To the Living God with whom the whole universe belongs.
He has everything you'll ever need for an abundantly, rich life.
So, why not put your total trust in Him since His promises are true and He never lies.

It is only through the One who is able to freely give
that your storehouse can be filled.
So, go to the One who is rich beyond imagination, who can make your life a thrill.
You can't do any better than going to the origin of The Source.
There is where you'll get all that counts like an eternal, flowing water fount.

Make it a point to be secure about all that you must have to survive and thrive.
Know without a doubt that your provision is in The Source, who is alive.
When it comes to being "full to running over", He don't jive.

Promises: Given The Charge

The charge to keep: to be morally and personally responsible
for your actions and reactions.
It is everyone's duty to do what is right.
The key to solving our human service problems is to exercise compassion
and follow-up with action.
We can't just have sympathy and continue steppin' along our merry way.
We should stop, listen, and help as we're able, to realize seeing brighter days.
Our society is ill 'cause too many are too self-centered with the exception of a few.
Time to turn about to do common good: take care of self, yeah,
but don't ignore those less fortunate than you.

Attitudes need to shift and maybe one day we'll see everyone
loving their neighbors as themselves.
Love and caring all around: this will be the promise realized
given the charge finds solid ground.

<u>*To Be Content*</u>

The simple necessities and pleasures of life are all I need to be content:
Family, a few true friends, security, and (most importantly) love.
Love is in all that is dear to the heart;
For without love, everything that is worth having would fall apart.

To be content is to be at peace with what I have and what I do;
And any increase in my resources will be great, too.
To be content is to have joy that can't be taken away ;
'cause it's from deep within, forever to stay.

The Wonder of True Love

A pure heart for people, an enduring love and gratefulness of my family and friends ;
it's the wonder of true love and I wouldn't trade it for anything.
Truly, the experience of caring so much for someone
that you feel a part of them is supernatural.
There are times of reflection that cause me to just sit still in awe
of being so blessed with those who affectionately surround me.
With support of family & friends, you can persevere
through all that life brings your way.
So strive to continually strengthen your bind, day by day.

What has happened in our present? Love doesn't seem
to be expressed nearly enough as I heard about from my parents,
during their childhood.
I know the reasons that have been discussed and agree with the consensus —
a lack of sufficiency in "proven values."
"Proven Values" – believing and practicing the simple, profound principles of community living.
Since there is a gap in the wonder of true love, only a decided few carry the "weight."
Problem? Yes, the load is progressively becoming too heavy to bear.
So, we all need to assess our resources and then, as able, share.

The wonder of true love, unconditional love, is intense ;
but if exercised right, it will last.
It is imperative to capture the revelation of the power of true love
And then use it in all our social interaction.
Start the outpouring and just let it flow.
When it has been released, then we'll have reached a goal:
to touch deeply causing it to spread like wildfire,
to transform one's spirit to reach higher;
to affect change in life on Earth,
only true love will prevail in conquering past, present, and future challenges birthed.

True Love. Peace. Harmony.
Go for it and hold it upright,
So that you can have relations that will be a delight.

A Lesson Learned

What happens on the outside affects the inside and vice versa.
The affect: it can't be hidden because it's evident and strong.
I went through the testing once before and came out only slightly sore.
The lesson to be learned – absolute trust in God.
I thought I had it down, but no 'cause time #2 came around.

Once again, as I now know without thought,
All the answers are with The One Above, my best clout.
The lesson learned – in His strength, I determine to steadily run my course.
Thank you Lord for your " full-proof" faithfulness in being My Source.

Reality

The foundation of personal development is to be given by parents,
the start: at home.
And then from there, there are other influences which shape
How we become known.
Despite similarities that you may find with peers,
uniqueness eventually shows clear.
One common interest that all people do have is faith or hope
in something and/or someone.
For we all have our limits of what we, alone, can get done.
And one common fact is: everyone that knows or meets you will not like you.
Why? Differences sometimes never mesh.
So, as best as we can, we live at peace with all
and keep our attitudes positively fresh.

Within, be free.
Love yourself and always a good result you'll see.
Acceptance of who you are and how you desire to grow
is the only way to let people know you're secure in your self-identity.
And so reality is qué será será — whatever will be, will be.

Outside To Inside

By birth, life begins ; by environment, growth from within.
Have to find nutrients to keep nurturing, keep nurturing, keep nurturing.
I'm me, you're you, they're them.

Life is a mix of variables: people, places, events, things.
How life goes for you is more than what to it you bring.
What happens beyond one's self-control?
The best route: "go with the flow."

What's most important is what's on the inside.
Outside to inside, outside to inside, listen:
"We're one in spirit. Let nothing break our esteem ; remember, we're a team."

Keep Your Dreams Alive

A dream or dreams: that certain aspiration that if realized
will give you a great sense of warm jubilance.
Everyone who dares to dream usually does so without boundaries,
but at times, one exception — lack of determination — this is the tragedy of many dreams;
and sadly, they end up washed out in downstreams.
Don't let your dreams hang out to dry.
If you have a dream or dreams, go for it —
knowing that success only comes with a relentless try, try, try.

It doesn't matter how long it takes, a perfect example is Rev. Dr. Martin Luther King.
He was taken from us, but his spirit and vision are being kept alive to loudly ring.
So, take advantage of being alive; strive, strive, strive.
No, it's not easy to live life and dream dreams;
it requires discipline, energy, and wisdom — all of them requiring time.
Yet, I earnestly challenge me & you;
get your tools together, use them, and make your dreams come true.

Faithful Companion

Wherever I am, wherever I go, whenever I need Him,
my Faithful Companion is always beside me.
Ever since he introduced himself to me, He's been everything I ever needed
and wanted in a Best Friend: a comforter, compassionate, genuine, and loving.
Even when, every now and then, concerns about life
weigh heavy on my mind, He's there to make the carrying lighter,
for He says "all that regards you is mine."
He's a great teacher;
He repeatedly reveals to me truths of priceless value, lessons to exercise.

My Faithful Companion never stops cheering me on to attaining The Prize.
And the greatest fact of all,
my Faithful Companion never has or will remove His presence from me.
For in His essence, I'm being molded to be.

Listen Up, Youth

God's love is pure and waiting for you to receive.
If you only are hip and tuff enough to totally trust Him,
the greatest wealth of all — His riches will be yours indeed.

Be bold and be always striving to "do the right thing."
For if you do so, His joy, love, and strength in your heart,
He will bring.

Word.

You Can't Understand, But Maybe...

As much as lies within your intellect and sympathy,
You can't always understand why and how things happen.
There are some things, in time, that you'll be able to comprehend.
Then, there are other things which can only be handled from another end.

The whys to not understanding:

You can't understand unless you really realize the affects of the facts.
You can't understand unless you've tread in "the event tracks."
But maybe, if you avoid assuming and wondering at all,
You can learn a new way to be wise:
by keeping everything in line with supernatural, spiritual eyes.

On The Word

Honor and self-respect is a building process that we all work to have and keep.
We learn standards to guide us on the straight and narrow paths,
where we seek to be swift on our feet.
It's not difficult when all is "peachy keen,"
but watch out when rough periods make turbulent what was serene.
Beware lest ye fall by your actions and/or speech;
for by them, consequences will unfold that won't always be sweet.

That's, why despite the actuality of temporary weakness,
I declare: "Standing On The Word!!!"
There is no other option but truth to sustain
so that perfect peace can remain.

On The Word, On The Word, there's no other way to joyfully go.
On The Word, On The Word, from you let it vivaciously glow.

Going Home

"There's no place like home." For me, so true; is it for you?
For me, the place where family grows closer,
where laughter, joy, peace, and creating memories is ongoing.
It's the place where unconditional love is continually flowing.

For a season, I'm home again.
When I knew I was going home,
My soul was comforted, knowing that it was the right move.
I look forward to really getting set with all that I must do,
So I'll be able to achieve being well-established
and go on to all that's new.

What's Your Worth?

It is an invaluable treasure and unique, too.
It is life, yours; yeah, you.
In the Creator's view, you're an apple of His eye.
Your plan to be whatever you want to be is not an unattainable high.
If you journey diligently and consistently work hard,
you'll have no problem with going far.
So what if you make mistakes —"too err is human";
accept and learn from them, avoid repeating them again.

What's your worth? Your life has purpose that is immeasurable.
So, find your calling;
And when you get it, go "with the strength."

Go Forth

Get up, get going, go forth.

The past can't be changed; lived, it's gone.
The present; it's on you to decide what to do.
The future; only God knows.
The options of destination are: stay where you are
and make no effort to move
or go forth, get in your groove.

You can pass all your "tests"; just do your part,
and God will take care of the rest.
Go boldly, therefore, unto the throne of grace.
Don't wait, there's no time to waste.
Life is too short to worry, to let any good opportunity pass by.
So, always be ready, step forward, your time is nigh.

Simple?

"Ye shall know the truth
and the truth shall set you free" — simple?

Eat, exercise, and rest well, you'll increase your chance
to live long — simple?

Be yourself, live for your happiness;
only God can change you for the better — simple?

Be cheerful in giving, humble, and learn longsuffering ;
your blessings will abound — simple?

Take advantage of good choices, secure your path — simple?

The Greatest Joy

There is an assurance that is so great
that nothing can break its bind.
It is so comforting that it soothes —
giving perfect peace of mind.
This assurance is the greatest joy in the world;
it's knowing that you have a special, personal relationship with Jesus.
There is nothing more precious — not anything, anywhere.

So why not check out this most worthy acquaintance;
don't mind those who may or will call you "square."
It's your life, next to The Creator, you know what's best for you.
So, I dare you; give Jesus some time
and see if what I've said is true.
If you give this dare a chance, I'm sure you'll agree:
"Jesus is the best thing that ever happened to thee."

Everlasting

There are a few things that will last forever:
unconditional love, acts of humanity, life and death — that's about it?
And all these things are overseen by One Mighty One —
The Living God, creator of Heaven and Earth.

What is truly everlasting is eternal life.
Think about that — eternal life.
Only one way to secure it and that's through Jesus Christ.
Get to know Him and thoroughly enjoy the invested time of immense appeal.
Give this decision serious consideration;
be open and humble to what it provides.
Then be mindful, that once you make your choice,
in it joyously abide.

Along The Shore

On good weather days, I love to go along the shore on my bicycle –
pedaling at a steady pace.
It's a time of refreshment,
especially when the wind wisping over my face.

I observe, in amazement, the crispness of the surrounding scenery:
the clear blue sky, the reflections of the sun –
their colors, the greenery.

And I say to myself: "Mm, beautiful!"
The sweet serenity is beyond compare.
And especially on a quiet day or night,
you'll see it's a precious creation of care.

Community Service Theme

Part One:

Let's go team, let's make the move;
Time to work, get in our groove.
We've got much to do, indeed;
Service with love, we aim to please.
Sound Off: 1,2
Sound Off: 3,4
Sound Off: 1,2,3,4
Let's do it!!!

Part Two:

That's it team, we made the move;
Went to work, got in our groove.
We did much, oh yes, indeed;
Service with love, we did it with ease.
Sound Off: 1,2
Sound Off: 3,4
Sound Off: 1,2,3,4
We did it!!!

A Vision Of Hope

The world we live in is the scope.
We must act now if we're to experience a vision of hope.
Youth be youth: stop the violence, the drugs, the forecasted genocide.
Go back to hoops: friendly style, New York, too;
hang out with family and friends, be yourself, good clean fun — that's cool.

Adults be nurturers, pump high confidence and encouragement into "your kids."
Lend a helping hand as you can.
Take time, now vs. later;
it will be a great reward — sowing good seed into fertile land.

We, the community, must come together.
Time to put differences aside; time to build a collective wealth.
We can't just go for self.
We must be about self-empowerment/self-love, yes;
but we must also share when we've "arrived", been blessed.

So, wadda ya say? Let's get busy to do great works for the benefit of us all.
Let's grow strong and rich so we can keep the cycle goin',
and one by one, stand mighty tall.

Make the Better Choice

There are only two kinds of choices to make: good and bad,
and the subset of those two choices: better and best.
It's not always possible to make the best choice,
but it's very much in everyone's ability to make the better choice.
So, here's a few examples to test;
make the better choice and do your best:

Live by faith or live by sight? Make the better choice.

Live to acquire an abundance of material valuables
or live to have riches beyond value; family, friends,
joy, health, peace? Make the better choice.

Be humble and then be exalted or be prideful and fall hard?
Make the better choice.

Soldier the good fight of faith or give in to unbelief?
Make the better choice.

Try to do everything your way or do everything through divine guidance?
Make the better choice.

Hunger and thirst after righteousness and eternal life
or do what feels good not knowing the expected end?
Make the better choice.

Hope you did your best and made the better choices.
Time will surely tell.

I Am That I Am

Yahweh (Hebrew) – The Lord Is One,

Alpha and Omega – The Beginning and The End.

The greatest power of all;

so why not lay your life in His hands?

Yehovah (M'Kaddesh, Nissi, Rohi, Rophe, Shalom, Shammah, Tsidkenu, Yireh).

Halleluyah!!!

"Whatever you need me to be, I can be," says Yahweh.

I Am That I Am.

I Am That I Am is all in all and owns all of all.

So seek Him out;

See that He's about truth,

His Word and actions are proof.

The Power, all that there is, is I Am That I Am.

The Light

It was more than 2,000 years ago when a baby named Jesus was born.

And every December 25th, those who love Him celebrate His birth;

reflecting on hope to see true peace on Earth.

Why did He come? —

to re-establish our connection to The Father which had been undone.

Yes, Jesus is The Light and we need to be mindful

to maintain the true perspective of this holiday season —

giving of self to others, sharing, reminiscing, giving thanks for life.

If you don't have now or ever have any material "jewels",

it's no big deal.

The richest free-of-cost "jewel" is The Light,

who is real.

Victory

More power to us, when victory comes through trust.

Victory — triumph that can't be denied;

Walk in it with humble pride.

Victory, you can have it in your life.

How much of it depends on how well you live right.

Take your steps, carefully;

get a rhythm with smooth flow.

And soon, you'll be swiftly movin', an example to show.

Be encouraged, be of good cheer;

with courage in your corner, you have nothing to fear.

So claim victory over every situation that arises.

Do your part; but more readily, be guided.

<u>R.E.A.C.H.</u>

Resilience
Enjoyment
Aspiration
Compassion
Hope

Acquire
&
Hold Onto Them

Affordable Funky Threads

I am a 6'1" African-American woman.
And when I meet people at social events, I often receive the comments:
"I like what you're wearing. Where did you buy it and do you ever have trouble
finding clothes that fit well?
These are revolving questions, but I always respond respectively:
"Thank you! At_____ or it was a gift, and honestly no."
You may not share this particular scenario about fashion wear with me;
but what about finding funky threads that are affordable?

Do you find that they tend to be expensive in high-end retail stores?
I have found this to be generally true.
Nonetheless, in my determined spirit to be frugal and purchase only stylish wear,
There are a few places where I regularly find great buys:
Filene's Basement, The Limited, Marshall's and various boutique shops
including Allston Beat, Bushwear, The Garment District,
and a few stores in Cambridgeside Galleria Mall.
These are places to check out.

When it comes to fashion, there is one very important truth
that must be upheld (and I, myself, do uphold it) –
only buy what you like that suits you well.
You should not dress to please others or necessarily acquire "what's the in thang."
In my opinion, all clothing is "what's in."
There is something for everyone, but not everything for everyone.
So, be unique in your "flair affair";
and remember, always buy what's "funky good" for you.

From The Heart

From The Heart, purity;
from the heart, creativity.

From The Heart, you own;
from the heart, nothing is for loan.

From The Heart, you're bare;
from the heart, develops your "love affair."

From The Heart, all is well;
from the heart, you have a legacy to tell.

Tell Your Legacy Well.

The Strength Within

There is no power that can match 'The Strength Within."
With it, through every test of life, it's your closest kin.

It's physical, emotional, mental, and spiritual health.
Within each person, The Strength Within is a characteristic of one's self.

Anytime you need "The Strength Within" to rise, you can call on it
and let it lead you, over and through.

Oh, what a reserve of vitality you have at your fingertips.
To access it, just believe and then request it from your lips.

What Up?

When you hear what God can do and more so who He is,
how do you live without Him?

Don't you have any sense of the dangers of daily life?
If you're not protected by God's favor,
any day at any time could become sourly savored.

So, which way will you choose — up or down?
Be mindful and answer the question, What up?
And when you answer, may your response be:
"God, that's what up!

Check Thine Self

Every moment, every day, check thine self.
Who you are, how you appear, the way you do things;
It all should be done in decency and order.
When you make a mistake at any time, "stop, evaluate, rectify."
With God as your source, help is always nigh.

Progress. You must persevere
to become a master in making what is weak, strong.
Don't give up, no matter how tough the issue;
hang tight, hold on.

Learn from all the experiences in your life;
steadily pursue excellence, day and night.

Justice

A Higher Power that is above the courts and law,
where true justice comes from —It's with The One.

To right the wrongs of our society,
we must invest in and use all resources available.
Then, the payoff of all the investment will propel
the "effort wave," richly enable.

Ultimately, the final frontier of justice being done
is with God above, whose final word is "Won."

All Of Me

If you want to be with me, you have to be with all of me.
You said, when I made a commitment to You, "surrender all."
And so, I commenced to give you all of me —
from the crown of my head to the soles of my feet.

I'm all yours.
Take and fill me with your sweet Spirit 'til I'm full.
Then, I'll empty out and start over again and again...
And in this place of submission,
I'm able to be abased and to abound.

Nothing to hold me back, I'll always move forward
to be my best and nothing less.
All of me, all of me,
purposed to be the best I can be.

Give It To Me Straight

Ya know, I am so tired of politicians making promises they don't keep
and not keeping themselves accountable to the people
that they're suppose to be representin'.
Don't get me wrong. There are a few "politicians"
who do their job and do it well.
But, these are not politicians rather they are concerned citizens
and community activists who became so frustrated
with their elected officials that they ran for office and were elected.
This is what we need: people who are truly committed
to the betterment of our communities and surrounding neighborhoods.

The other side of "the political action coin" is apathy
on the part of citizens who are eligible to vote.
If the eligible don't register and vote,
they don't have a right to complain about anything that's not happenin'.
People have got to realize that the power to change
For the benefit of everyone is in our individual/collective hands.
'Cause it's true that "one person can make a difference."

So, let's stop beating around the bush of complacency
We've all got to be active in ensuring
that we have a future to live in, productively.

Moving Right Along

Have you ever wanted something to hurry up and happen
(e.g. can't wait for the weekend, your birthday, a staff meeting to end)?
Well, I've identified a phrase that is applicable;
and when used it works: MRA (Moving Right Along).

In whatever, "let's get to it situation," this can be used
to shorten what might otherwise be long.
It's important to use MRA because it assures efficiency and productivity.

So, always be verbally armed when going into tedious activities.
With MRA, there's no nagging delays.

Remain With Me

"Abide in me, and I in you and we'll bear much fruit;
for apart from me, you can do nothing."
This is what God says do, for me and you.
In Him is where we need to abide.
And, we must stand correct with each other in relationships which are right.

If you can't be for real, be sincere, please don't be a part of my life;
'cause I don't want any unnecessary heartache or any other strife.

So, think before you decide: is it worth it to pursue?
Remember, when you make a promise/vow, God and the recipient
expect you to follow through.
With God, family, and friends, the desire is "remain with me."
To be fruitful, real, sincere, you must always be open and free.

An Eagle's Mind

One of our most precious endangered species, The American Bald Eagle,
is beauty in flight and when still.
Its inhabitance is always high up in the mountains or the hills.
So graceful, so smooth, eagles love to cruise.

What I admire most about the eagle is its courage
and pursuit to fly to the highest peaks.
No matter what appears, at times, to block their way;
They find the energy to get where they want to go.
Such strong character they have,
sure 'nuf a model to imitate.

So seriously ponder about developing such a mind — work and wait.

Talk To Me

"Who shall separate me from the love of Christ…"
You are a joyful spirit. Your desire — to live life to the hilt,
with God's direction.
But as with all of us, sometimes come distractions, sidetracks, setbacks.
And thus, you have to step up what became lack.
This doesn't happen because it's part of the original plan.
It's not a time to withdraw,
but rather get up and regroup from the fall.
Or, you know but don't do;
something went wrong due to action prolonged.

In every decision, in every action, take time to "Talk With Me."
God wants only the best for you.
So, be open to His counsel; no disappointments, He's true blue.

Become a member of the network that is larger than life itself.
Join the adopted family in which God says, "Talk To Me,
I'm Your Help."

The Ultimate Challenge

Have you ever been faced with the ultimate challenge in your life —
a dare to defend your faith, family, a friend, or values?
For me, it was my faith in Christ.
I knew I was grounded in The Word;
So I stood firm and used my spiritual armor to fight the good fight.

The conversation was intense and values & knowledge were shared.
The bottom line was answering the questions: What is the heart of the issue?
What is the foundation of your belief?

The time of mutual agreement came and the final word was said.
And, we parted thanking God that we had The Truth;
respect, love, and friendship remained intact.

On My Way

Assertive. Attentive. Believing. Committed.
These are my A's, B, and C to alternate: learn, teach, learn…

I'm ordinary here, I'm exceptional there;
on my way.
One rung at a time, gonna reach my prime;
on my way.
Trekin' at a steady clip, carefully watchin' not to trip;
on my way.

No time to judge, no time to pout;
Keep focus ahead, can't be misled.
It ain't about where I was,
It ain't about where I'm at,
It's about where I'm going.
Despite any cynicism, I'm solid in knowing —
success is ongoing.

We all have the means.
So, let's head out on our way.

Forthcoming Collections
By: M.D. Smith

- ❖ _Quench The Thirst_ © 1998
- ❖ _Heritage Quilt_ © 1999
- ❖ _Positioned and Blessed_ © 2000
- ❖ _Next Steps, New Heights_ © 2003
- ❖ _New Beginnings_ © 2005

Final Note

If you enjoyed any segment of this book and/or have any questions or thoughts,
please share with me

or

If you are affiliated with a non-profit organization and would like to use this book
as a fundraising tool and keep 100% of the proceeds,
contact me
@
mdsmith@MissionPossibleCollaborative.com.